Y

MISHAWAKA-PENN-HARRIS PUBLIC LIBRARY

P9-AQB-321

BITTERSWEET

Character Education

Leadership

by Lucia Raatma

Consultant:
Madonna Murphy, Ph.D.
Professor of Education
University of St. Francis, Joliet, Illinois
Author, *Character Education in America's Blue Ribbon Schools*

Bridgestone Books
an imprint of Capstone Press
Mankato, Minnesota

Mishawaka-Penn-Harris
Public Library
Mishawaka, Indiana

Bridgestone Books are published by Capstone Press
151 Good Counsel Drive, P.O. Box 669, Mankato, Minnesota 56002
http://www.capstone-press.com

Copyright © 2003 by Capstone Press. All rights reserved.
No part of this publication may be reproduced in whole or in part, or stored in a retrieval
system, or transmitted in any form or by any means, electronic, mechanical, photocopying,
recording, or otherwise, without written permission of the publisher.
For information regarding permission, write to Capstone Press,
151 Good Counsel Drive, P.O. Box 669, Dept. R, Mankato, Minnesota 56002
Printed in the United States of America.

Library of Congress Cataloging-in-Publication Data
Raatma, Lucia.
    Leadership / by Lucia Raatma.
    p. cm.—(Character education)
    Includes bibliographical references and index.
    Summary: Explains the virtue of leadership and describes ways to be a leader
in the home, school, and community.
    ISBN 0-7368-1389-6 (hardcover)
    1. Leadership—Juvenile literature. [1. Leadership.] I. Title. II. Series.
BF723.L4 R33 2003
158′.4—dc21   2001007906

Editorial Credits

Megan Schoeneberger, editor; Karen Risch, product planning editor; Steve Christensen,
    series designer, Heidi Meyer, book designer; Alta Schaffer, photo researcher;
    Nancy White, photo stylist

Photo Credits

Capstone Press/Jim Foell, cover, 8, 10, 16, 20
CORBIS/Bettmann, 18
Diane Meyer, 14
PhotoDisc, Inc., 12
Skjold Photographs, 4, 6

1 2 3 4 5 6 07 06 05 04 03 02

Table of Contents

Leadership

Good leaders inspire people to do their best. Leadership is about being a good role model. Leaders help people get work done together. But leadership never is about being bossy. Leaders help others accomplish their goals.

inspire
to give someone a feeling or an idea

Being a Leader

Many leaders in your life are adults. Some leaders are in charge of groups of people. Other leaders are the first to achieve a goal. These leaders show the way for others to follow. You also can be a leader. You can start a music club and plan a musical recital at your school.

recital
a show where people sing or
play a musical instrument for others

Leadership at Home

You can be a leader with your family members. Set a good example by following rules. You also can teach your family to play a game. A good leader chooses a game everyone can play together.

Leadership with Your Friends

Every group of friends has leaders and followers. Leaders plan fun games for their friends. They choose fair teams. They also help solve disagreements. Leaders listen to everyone's ideas before making a decision.

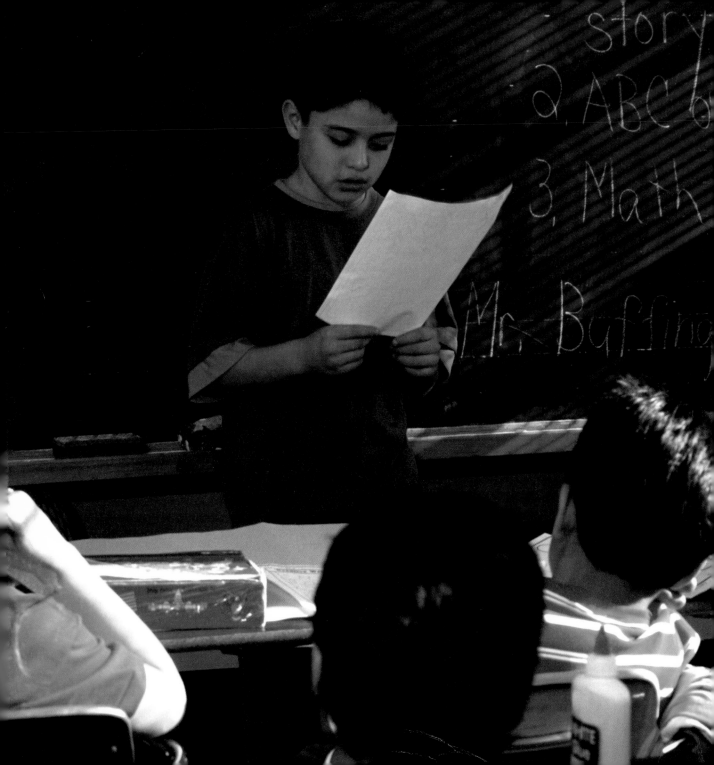

Leadership at School

Groups at school need leaders. Some leaders organize school plays and games. Leaders give out jobs for group members to do. Other leaders start the lines that lead students to lunch. Some leaders offer to read out loud in class.

organize
to plan and run an event

Leadership in Sports

Team leaders set a good example for other players on the team. Team leaders follow the rules. They make sure that everyone gets a chance to play. Leaders encourage team members to play together fairly and have fun.

encourage
to give praise and support

Leadership in Your Community

Your community has many leaders.
You can be a leader in your community
too. You can recycle aluminum cans
and newspapers from your neighbors.
Show leadership by helping to plant
trees and flowers at the park.

"Women must try to do things as men have tried. When they fail, their failure must be but a challenge to others."
—Amelia Earhart

Amelia Earhart

Amelia Earhart was one of the first women to fly an airplane. In 1932, she flew her plane across the Atlantic Ocean. She was the first woman to make this trip. Amelia inspired people from all over the world. Many men and women became pilots because of her leadership.

pilot
a person who flies an airplane

Leadership and You

You can be a good leader. Listen to other people in your group. Remember that you cannot always take the lead. All groups have leaders and followers. Good followers help their leaders. Good leaders and followers earn respect from others in the group.

Hands On: Follow the Leader

A simple game on the playground can teach you about leadership. You can see what it is like both to lead and to follow.

What You Need

A group of friends
A playground

What You Do

1. Choose one person to be the leader. The leader looks around the playground and makes a plan of what he or she is going to do.
2. Followers line up behind the leader.
3. The leader then goes through the playground. He or she may climb up steps and go down a slide. The leader then may crawl through a tunnel on the play gym.
4. The leader must think of those following him or her. The leader should not do anything unsafe.
5. The followers follow the leader wherever they are led.
6. Each person in the group can have a turn at being the leader.

Talk to your friends when you are finished. Ask who liked leading and who liked following. Which did you like better?

Words to Know

achieve (uh-CHEEVE)—to do something successfully, especially after a lot of effort

encourage (en-KUR-ij)—to give praise and support; a good leader encourages everyone in a group.

goal (GOHL)—something that you aim for; leaders help others achieve their goals.

inspire (in-SPIRE)—to give someone a feeling or an idea; leaders inspire others to be successful.

role model (ROHL MOD-uhl)—someone who sets a good example for others; being a good role model means following rules and making safe choices.

Read More

Cefrey, Holly. *Everything You Need to Know about the Art of Leadership: How to Be a Positive Influence in Your Home, School, and Community.* The Need to Know Library. New York: Rosen, 2000.

Rosenthal, Marilyn S., and Daniel B. Freeman. *Amelia Earhart: A Photo-Illustrated Biography.* Photo-Illustrated Biographies. Mankato, Minn.: Bridgestone Books, 1999.

Internet Sites

Amelia Earhart Birthplace Museum
http://www.ameliaearhartmuseum.org
Crossroads of Character
http://library.thinkquest.org/J001675F/?tqskip=1
Learning about Leadership
http://www.pinetreeweb.com/whatis.htm

Index